COMPACTS are very different from every other type of adventure game book. They have been specially designed so that their play is as convenient as possible.

Your score cards are on special fold-out flaps, so your current score will always be there at a glance. These flaps also contain all your *adventure accessories*. The only thing you have to provide yourself is a pen or pencil to mark your score card.

You don't even need an eraser because there are enough score cards (a whole 40!) to allow for a fresh one to be used for each new game.

COMPACTS are ideal for playing at home, on holiday, in the car . . . wherever you like!

Haunted Island

Illustrated by Peter Dennis

HODDER AND STOUGHTON
LONDON SYDNEY AUCKLAND

British Library Cataloguing in Publication Data

A catalogue record for this book is available from the British Library

ISBN 0 340 58859 4

Published by Hodder and Stoughton Children's Books,
a division of Hodder and Stoughton Ltd,
Mill Road, Dunton Green, Sevenoaks, Kent TN13 2YA

Photoset by Rowland Phototypesetting Ltd,
Bury St Edmunds, Suffolk

Printed in Great Britain by Biddles Ltd,
Guildford and King's Lynn

◇ THE ADVENTURE ◇

Just your luck! All your friends have landed jobs with the nearby theme park for the summer vacation. But what was the only holiday job YOU could find? Helping out some boring museum curator somewhere miles away, at the ends of the earth!

At least, the little village *feels* like the ends of the earth after your long journey to it. In fact, it is just over a hundred miles away from your home – but the desolation of the place makes those hundred miles seem more like a thousand.

But you are soon wondering whether you were quite so unfortunate to find this job after all. George Drabb is the curator's name – but if drab by name, he certainly isn't by nature. A fattish little man, he wears the most outlandish tie and pair of spectacles you've ever seen! And his manner is brisk and excitable.

'I hope you're not expecting a lazy time filling out filing cards,' he says the moment he meets you. 'I placed that advertisement for a young assistant for one reason and one reason only. So I'll have someone to come with me to the island to help with my search!'

You're puzzled. 'What island? What search?' you ask.

'The tiny island ten miles south-west of here,' he answers eagerly. 'Just off the coast – and once the stronghold of the Fothering family. Still doesn't mean anything to you? To me neither until a few weeks ago! You see, I've only just been transferred down here.

Anyway, the Fotherings' castle was quite impregnable because of the treacherous rocks guarding the island. Of course, the castle's in ruins now.'

'So what exactly would we be searching for amongst these ruins?'

The curator's eyes shine even brighter behind his spectacles. 'A treasure quite priceless, that's what!' he exclaims. 'A set of sixteenth-century solid gold goblets! Here, read this,' he adds breathlessly, unlocking one of the museum's display cases and handing you a yellowed roll of parchment.

'But it's in Latin,' you remark. 'I only know the odd word.'

'Same with most people. That's why its story has remained untold all this time. The parchment has been stared at in this case for years and years but it seems that no one has bothered to try and translate it until I came along!'

'So what is its story?'

'The parchment relates the castle's great tragedy some four hundred years ago,' he says. 'The owner then was Sir Henry Fothering who had a beautiful daughter, Isabella. He'd arranged for her to marry the lord of one of the castles further up the coast and he commissioned five solid gold goblets to be made for her dowry. But Isabella was in love with a young minstrel at the castle and the pair of them hid the goblets around the island in the hope that it would stop the marriage.'

'Did it?' you ask eagerly, becoming more and more interested.

'In a way,' the curator replies sadly. 'When Sir Henry found out about his daughter's disobedience he fell into a mad rage and pursued her up on to the battlements of the castle. There was a terrible storm that night and she suddenly slipped and tragically fell to her doom. Sir Henry was so broken-hearted that he spent the rest of his years living on the island completely alone.'

'And you reckon the goblets have never been found?'

'Not according to this parchment. But I have every confidence that we three can find them!'

'*Three?*' you ask, puzzled.

'Oh yes, I forgot to introduce you to my dog, Cheerful.' He whistles in the direction of the adjoining room, but it is only after quite some time that Cheerful responds, eventually plodding in with the most miserable face you've ever seen. Talk of hangdog. His jowls and drooping lower eyelids nearly touch the floor!

'Now, let's get down to that part of the coast right away, shall we?' Mr Drabb says, after affectionately patting the impassive dog. 'There's a fisherman living just opposite the island whom I've managed to persuade to row us across.'

It's only when you arrive at the fisherman's cottage that you discover there were a couple of little things the curator omitted to tell you about the desolate island. First, because the jutting rocks are only safe when completely submerged at high tide, the voyage across can't be made until dusk. And second, he omitted to tell you about the many local tales of *ghosts* that roam the island's shores!

◇ GAME INSTRUCTIONS ◇

1. For each attempt at the game, you must use one of the 40 score cards on the inside of the book's fold-out flaps. So your score card is as handy as possible during the game, always keep the appropriate flap *opened out* as you read through the book. (Right-handed readers will find it more convenient to use the score cards at the back of the book first, and left-handed readers those at the front.)

2. The ♥ column on your score card is for showing *the number of ghosts you encounter*, the ♟ column *the number of goblets you have found* and the ◆ column which *accessories* you have collected.

♥ Column

3. Your nerves can stand up to **4** ghost encounters in all – and so **4** is the number of chances you're given in this column. As soon as you experience a haunting during the game, you must amend the ♥ column to show that you then have one chance less. You do this by using a pen or pencil to delete the **1**. If you later experience another haunting, you delete the **2** to show that another chance has gone . . . and so on.

4. When you have deleted every number down to and including **4**, this means you have been scared completely out of your wits and so must immediately end your search of the island. If you wish to make another attempt at the game, you must start

◇ GAME INSTRUCTIONS ◇

all over again from the beginning (using a fresh score card).

♟ Column

5. The object of the game is not only to avoid too many hauntings and therefore reach the end of the story, but also to find as many of the hidden goblets as possible. If you discover a goblet during the game, show this on your score card by circling the **1** in the ♟ column with a pen or pencil. If you discover another, circle the **2** and so on.

6. The more times you attempt the game, the better your final *goblets* score should be. Only when you have collected the maximum of five goblets in one game (i.e. found the whole set) has your search of Haunted Island been a total success!

✎ Column

7. There are three useful *accessories* to be picked up during the game: a map, a scroll and a book of crests. These are depicted on the outside of the book's fold-out flaps. Possession of these accessories will greatly improve your chances of a successful search and so you should make every effort to find them during the game.

8. If you *do* pick up one of the accessories, show this on your score card by circling that accessory's initials (M = Map, S = Scroll, B = Book of Crests)

in the ✍ column. This means that you are then entitled to consult this particular accessory where appropriate during the game. On such occasions, simply fold in the appropriate flap so the accessory you need is next to the part you're reading.

9. Any accessory not circled on your score card may NOT be folded over and consulted at any point during the game.

*You are now ready to start
your mission. Good luck . . .*

'Don't expect me to wait for you,' the fisherman mumbles as he rows you towards the forbidding outcrop. The island rises dark from the turbulent sea, the castle's ruins a jagged silhouette at its top. 'I'll come back for you in exactly five hours' time,' the fisherman adds. 'I'd like my payment now, though . . . just in case.' Mr Drabb laughs heartily as he takes out his wallet. 'Oh, don't tell me you're another one who thinks that there are ghosts roaming the island!' he exclaims. 'You ought to be ashamed of yourself!' But the grumpy fisherman is still insistent on his early payment. And as the eerie island comes nearer, you can't say you completely blame him. The rock is brooding and sombre and you're sure you hear the occasional cry from its rugged shore. 'Oh, they're just seagulls!' Mr Drabb says, chuckling at your anxiety. 'Now, why don't you decide which of us three is to step ashore *first* when we land there?'

If choose yourself   **go to 115**
If choose Cheerful   **go to 78**
If choose Mr Drabb   **go to 56**

2

These thirty paces all but lead you back into the tower again. You're just a couple of metres short of that dark passageway. You wonder if you should continue those extra few metres. You can certainly find no sign of one of the goblets where you are now! But you realise that this is all just hopeful guesswork – and a waste of valuable time. So you resign yourselves to having to forget about that little drawing. You'll just have to hope that there are easier clues later on! It's then that you sense something hovering a short distance above your little group. Praying that it's just an owl, you nervously lift your head . . . *Go to 157*.

3

Ignoring these two passages leading off from the tower, your little group climbs higher and higher up the dark steps. You eventually reach the top, stepping outside into the fierce wind. As the storm still shudders over the island, fiery purple streaks lighting the sky, you catch a glimpse of some cliffs slightly over to your right. You can just make out a pair of caves at their base. If you were able to locate these on a map, you would have a much better idea of your bearings.

If you have circled the M in the 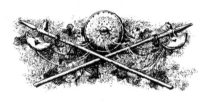 *column, you may consult the MAP accessory now to find out which square the pair of caves is in. If not, you'll have to guess:*

If you think B3	*go to 110*
If you think A3	*go to 48*
If you think A2	*go to 138*

4

Your guess at the secret instruction was obviously wrong. For you're only able to count out eighteen of the twenty-five paces before you reach the far end of the keep! Since you can't *keep* making guesses at what the little picture meant – you mustn't forget that you have only five hours here! – you all decide to return to the tower's stairway. Your little party has just stepped inside that narrow passage again, however, when you hear a strange sound behind you. Is it just the wind weaving through the parapets . . . or could it be a ghost *sniggering* at your disappointment? **Go to 57**.

5

Mr Drabb must have been right about that white apparition being the distorted reflection of the moon. For the storm now eases slightly and the hazy shape disappears. As the storm has eased, you suggest that you all make your way back to those steps that lead to the castle. As you're returning to them, however, you're still a little anxious about that white haze you saw through the rainstorm. Yes, it might just have been caused by the moon. The problem is – there's absolutely no sign of the moon at the moment up in that thundery sky! *Go to 106*.

6

The wind becomes fiercer as you and Cheerful nervously start to follow Mr Drabb up the twisting steps. Or maybe Cheerful isn't as nervous as you. It's so hard to tell from that unchanging expression on his face! 'We will be able to find our way back to that little cove won't we, Mr Drabb?' you ask anxiously as you climb higher and higher. 'These might be those type of strange steps that return to somewhere different than their starting place! I must say, I'd feel much happier if we could mark the location of that cove on a map . . . '

If you have circled the M in the  column, you may consult the MAP accessory now to find out which square the cove is in. If not, you'll have to guess:

    If you think D4   go to 38
    If you think B4   go to 99
    If you think C4   go to 151

7

You've only just started counting these twenty paces to the left when you hear a noise behind you. 'Did you hear it as well, Mr Drabb?' you ask nervously. 'It sounded like someone clambering quietly up the cask we've just been looking at!' Mr Drabb *did* hear the noise as well, but he's not nearly as unnerved by it as you are. At least, he *pretends* not to be. 'Oh, it was probably just a rat scrambling over the cask,' he says dismissively. 'Not scared of rats, are you?' *No, you're not.* As long as it *is* just a rat. Feeling very anxious, you look over your shoulder to see if Mr Drabb was right . . . ***Go to 90***.

8

Arriving at a narrow window in the wall, you find your excuse! 'What's that strange rock formation I can see way down there, Mr Drabb?' you call out casually. 'Ah, that's called a sea stack,' he says when he has walked through the darkness to join you. He explains that it's where the sea has eaten through part of the cliffs, leaving a little bit isolated from the rest. 'It would probably be worth looking for it on a map, wouldn't it?' you ask. 'So we'd know which direction we're facing.' Your real reason for wanting to do this, of course, is so that you can keep Mr Drabb here a bit longer!

If you have circled the M in the 📖 column, you may

consult the MAP accessory now to find out which square the sea stack is in. If not, you'll have to guess:

> If you think E2   go to 51
>
> If you think E1   go to 68
>
> If you think E3   go to 14

9

Unfortunately, of course, you don't have a map. So you're unable to find out exactly how far away those two cannons are. Perhaps it's not so unfortunate after all, though. Looking for them on a map would have delayed you even more. It's far more important that you reach the bottom of these cliff steps as quickly as possible! You're just about to turn the next bend in the steps, however, when you hear someone climbing slowly up them towards you. Perhaps it's the fisherman. Perhaps he's already landed and has come looking for you. But that tread sounds far too light to be a human's . . . *Go to 176.*

10

Having called Mr Drabb over to join your inspection of this window on the left, you both start to feel around the deep recess. Suddenly, you can hear what sounds like the hooves of a galloping horse outside! 'Oh, it's probably just the gurgling of a stream down below,' Mr Drabb says dismissively. 'With all this rain having fallen, the stream would obviously be quite noisy.' You'll only accept this explanation, however, if you can actually *see* a stream down there. So you lean right into the window recess, peering out at the dark ground below . . . *Go to 28.*

11

Delete the top number in your score card's ♥ column to show that you have one less chance after this haunting. Go next to 88.

12

As you're all hurrying down the cliff steps, you suddenly wonder whether these are in fact the right ones for the cove. They might be another set of steps – leading to somewhere very different! If only you could *see* the cove below. But you can't. If it is down there, then for the moment it's hidden. But, as the mist clears a bit more, you're able to make out a pinnacle of rock straight ahead, sticking out of the sea just off the island. Locating this rock on a map should tell you whether you're heading in the right direction or not . . .

If you have circled the M in the ◆ column, you may consult the MAP accessory now to find out which square the pinnacle of rock is in. If not, you'll have to guess:

If you think C4   go to 104
If you think D4   go to 166
If you think E4   go to 63

13

Mr Drabb's torch eerily lights up the dark stone as you nervously follow him down the branch of steps to the right. At last the tunnel levels out but it still seems to run on and on. 'Surely we should be nearing the main part of the castle by now, Mr Drabb?' you ask, somewhat dubious. 'Perhaps the tunnel doesn't run in that direction after all!' But it's then that you arrive at a large cavern filled with wooden casks. ***Go to 120.***

14

Suddenly, you hear what sounds like someone cackling from the other end of the hall. You and Mr Drabb turn to each other in alarm and then both peer into the darkness in the direction of the noise, hoping that it's just Cheerful sneezing. It would certainly have to be a very *strange* sneeze, though! But if it *is* cackling, whose could it be? A jester who used to entertain in the banqueting hall? You and Mr Drabb slowly and anxiously start to shine your torches round the vast, shadowy hall . . . *Go to 153.*

15

You were right about it being a dungeon behind the door! For as you and Mr Drabb push open the heavy door with your shoulders, your torches immediately light up a rusting ball and chain on the filthy floor. There are also rows upon rows of chalk markings on the stone wall. 'These must have been made by some poor prisoner, chalking the number of days he spent down here!' you remark gloomily. *Go to 137.*

Delete the top number in your score card's ♡ *column to show that you have one less chance after this haunting. Go next to 123.*

17

The thirty paces to the left don't bring you to any treasure, but they *do* bring you to the very end of this sinister tunnel. You find yourselves at the foot of another series of steps: this, thankfully, leading not down but up! 'I still believe that little drawing on the dungeon door was the work of Isabella,' Mr Drabb remarks thoughtfully. 'Perhaps that was the only place in the castle where she and her minstrel boyfriend could meet; the code being to remind them of the shortest way *out* of this dark and confusing tunnel!' *Go to 43*.

18

After you've helped him remove the helmet section, Mr Drabb reaches right inside this suit of armour. But, sadly, he's unable to find anything lodged down there. You now decide to try the suit of armour on the left – but this too proves disappointing. You're just about to examine the middle figure when you hear shuffling behind you. To your immense relief, you discover that it's just Cheerful, padding forlornly over to join you. But then you hear another spine-chilling sound – the creaking of metal! Has that suit of armour you were looking at suddenly come to life? Trembling with terror, you both turn your eyes back to it . . . *Go to 70*.

19

Having walked up to the cooking pot furthest from the spit, you and Mr Drabb now prepare to lift it. You know that it's likely to be extremely heavy and so you stand one on either side of it, each grabbing one of the large handles. 'One . . . two . . . three . . . *heave*!' Mr Drabb shrieks. You've just raised the pot a few inches from the ground, however, when you suddenly hear a slow creaking sound behind you. It's that iron spit – it's starting to turn again! Nearly dropping the pot on your toes in fright, you both slowly look towards the spit to see who or *what* is doing the turning . . . **Go to 52.**

20

Being a bloodhound, perhaps Cheerful was the most obvious one to choose to lead the way back to the cove. But you can't help feeling that there's something unlucky-looking about him! It must be that doleful expression on his face. You're soon wondering whether Mr Drabb might be even more unlucky for you, however, because you and Cheerful follow him right to the edge of a huge, sheer-sided hole. A couple more steps and you would have all plunged to your doom! But at least you've found something that's likely to be marked on a map of the island . . .

If you have circled the M in the *column, you may consult the MAP accessory now to find out which square this hole is in. If not, you'll have to guess:*

     If you think D3   go to 140
     If you think E3   go to 95
     If you think D2   go to 114

Delete the top number in your score card's 👻 *column to show that you have one less chance after this haunting. Go next to 74.*

22

Since he sounds so eager about it, you decide to let Mr Drabb lead the way through these large, dusty quarters. He decides the most methodical way of exploring them is to start by walking all the way round, next to the walls. He stops for a moment, though, when he comes to the first window; a deep, narrow opening in the crumbling stone. 'Can you see that derelict little building just down there?' he asks, pointing out the window. 'I'm sure it's a chapel. I suppose the only way to be absolutely certain, though, is to look for it on a map of the island.'

If you have circled the M in the  column, you may consult the MAP accessory now to find out which square the chapel is in. If not, you'll have to guess:

   If you think D2   *go to 74*
   If you think D3   *go to 122*
   If you think C3   *go to 162*

23

Mr Drabb was right when he said that you could expect to find the castle's kitchen on this floor. For, as you make your way towards the bottom right corner of the vast shadowy hall, you come across a huge fireplace there. A sturdy spit stands in it – large enough surely to have turned a whole ox over the fire – and, nearby, three massive upturned cooking pots. They're of thick cast-iron and look just like those you always see witches sitting by in illustrations of gruesome fairy stories! *Go next to 142.*

24

Having returned to the tower's stairway again, you now decide to explore the *other* passage that leads off it – the one that leads in the other direction. It is very short but takes you out on to the high wall that joins the tower with the main part of the castle. You soon discover that much of this wall has collapsed, though, making that route impossible. So your little party will just have to return to ground level in order to reach the rest of the castle! ***Go to 138.***

25

As soon as you've counted your twentieth pace from the tapestry, you and Mr Drabb eagerly tap all over the wall there. You're searching for a loose part of the rough stone, a part that might come out and expose a secret cavity! 'Ah, here we are!' Mr Drabb suddenly exclaims, as he starts to jiggle free a small section of the wall several feet off the ground. 'Now what's that in this hole behind here?' ***Go to 139.***

26

'Do you think this cave will eventually lead right up into the castle?' Mr Drabb asks as you both enter the huge hole, tentatively shining your torches round. 'Perhaps it formed a secret escape route in case the castle was ever besieged. I know how we could probably check this. We could see if the cave is depicted on a map of the island. If it isn't, then it presumably *was* a secret route!'

If you have circled the M in the  *column, you may consult the MAP accessory now to find out which square this cave is in. If not, you'll have to guess:*

    If you think D3   go to 85
    If you think B3   go to 40
    If you think C3   go to 149

27

'Come on, you two!' Mr Drabb says eagerly as the fisherman's boat finally disappears into the gloomy distance. 'If we've only got five hours before he comes back for us, we'd better start exploring the island straightaway!' He switches on the torch he brought with him and immediately starts to lead the way to a series of rough steps cut into the cliffs at the back of the cove. You much less enthusiastically switch on your own torch, and start to follow . . . *Go to 136.*

28

Delete the top number in your score card's ♥ column to show that you have one chance less after this haunting. Go next to 51.

29

It's lucky that you tried only thirty paces to the left of the boulder and not thirty-one! For your thirtieth pace through the mist brings you right to the cliff edge – just one more step and you would have plunged to your doom! Given that this wasn't the case, however, you're actually quite pleased to have found the cliff edge. All you have to do now is keep following it until you reach those steps that descend to the cove. They in fact prove to be very close, but you've climbed down only a few of them when you all suddenly freeze. Either it's a very large seagull – or there's a ghost hovering just above you. Bodies trembling, nerves on end, you all slowly look up . . . *Go to 82*.

30

You hurry a little way to the *left* of the steps because you can just make out a dark shape there through the sweeping rain. You think it might be an old sheep shelter. 'Oh no, it's just a rusty cannon!' you exclaim. 'Sorry about that. We should have just kept going for the castle, shouldn't we!' You're all about to hurry back in that direction when Mr Drabb suddenly grabs hold of your sleeve. 'I've just had a thought!' he remarks excitedly. 'The barrel of this cannon would have been a perfect place for hiding one of the goblets!' ***Go to 160***.

31

Delete the top number in your score card's ♡ column to show that you have one less chance after this haunting. Go next to 118.

32

Your little party has just started to make its way down the tower's shadowy steps again when you suddenly hear a noise from the top. It sounds like someone shuffling! Although you're trembling from head to toe, you suggest you all return up there to investigate – just in case it's Isabella's ghost, trying to show you that one of the goblets *is* hidden there! **Go to 145.**

33

As you continue your climb down to the cove, the mist starts to clear again and you suddenly spot a comforting sight in the distance. It's the fisherman rowing back towards the island. But *is* the sight quite so comforting? For it looks as if the little boat might reach the cove well before you three do. You'd really hoped to be there first so the fisherman doesn't assume you'd met your doom and immediately leave the island again! Anxious, you try to work out how far away the little boat is. It's currently passing underneath two cannons right at the edge of the island. You could do with a map . . .

If you have circled the M in the 🖐 column, you may consult the MAP accessory now to find out which square the cannons are in. If not, you'll have to guess:

    If you think E4   go to 75
    If you think D4   go to 9
    If you think E3   go to 167

34

You tread slowly and methodically across the wooden floorboards, desperately trying to find one that's loose. This constant creaking that accompanies you around makes the place seem eerier than ever, however, so you're greatly relieved when Mr Drabb suddenly calls out to you to join him. *He* had chosen to examine the walls and it sounds from his excited tone as if he has found something there! So you hurry over to him. ***Go to 158.***

35

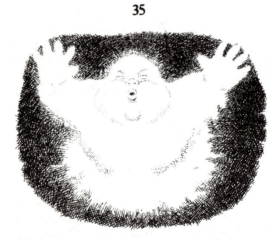

Delete the top number in your score card's ♡ column to show that you have one less chance after this haunting. Go next to 118.

36

The last few of these fifteen paces take you into that dark
passage again, back towards the tower. You and Mr
Drabb feel all over the rough stone here, your hands
desperately hoping to find a part that's loose and
concealing a secret cavity. It's eventually apparent,
though, that your guess at that secret instruction was
totally wrong. For the stone is completely sound in this
section of the passage. Perhaps you should have gone
fifteen paces to the *left* of that drawing instead. But
you've wasted enough time on this guessing game as it
is! You can't delay any more. *Go to 24.*

37

Having drawn the straw on the left, you anxiously wait
to see if either Mr Drabb's or Cheerful's is shorter.
Cheerful's isn't . . . but, to your great relief, his
master's *is*! Mr Drabb pretends that he doesn't mind at
all about this of course and immediately steps outside
the tower again. But you can't help noticing that his

torch is trembling a little as he does so. It's trembling a whole lot more when he returns to you both some twenty minutes later! ***Go to 164.***

38

'Of course these steps will take us back to the cove!' Mr Drabb says, laughing at you over his shoulder as he continues striding up them. 'How could they possibly not do? Now let's get one thing absolutely straight. There are no ghosts on this island and there's nothing strange or illogical about it!' As if to contradict him, however, something white suddenly starts to drift down towards you all from the darkness above. It looks like an arm. An arm in a loose white sleeve! Could it possibly be Isabella's arm, drifting down here to warn you against your exploration? Or are you letting your imagination run away with you? Perhaps it's just a seagull. You wait for whatever it is to come closer . . . ***Go next to 53.***

You knew that you should have hurried well away from this terrible place. For you're inspecting the manacle on the right when the dungeon door suddenly starts to close again! You all dash over to it and just manage to squeeze out in time. 'How on earth did that happen?' Mr Drabb asks, rather uncomfortably, as your little party continues along this underground passage. 'It was almost as if someone had been pulling the door from outside!' And perhaps you're now about to *see* that someone! For you all slowly turn in terror as you hear mischievous chuckling behind you . . . *Go to 16.*

'We're going to have to get moving, Mr Drabb,' you urge him after briefly and unsuccessfully searching the cave. 'There's only a quarter of an hour to go now before the fisherman is due back at the cove!' Fortunately, it's not much longer before you reach the cliff steps again.

But, as you're all hurrying down them, Mr Drabb suddenly stops. White as a sheet, he tells you that something has just tapped him on the shoulder! You anxiously turn round to see what it was, praying that it's just a long piece of bracken or another plant growing out of the rocks . . . *Go to 112*.

41

Since counting twenty-five paces to the *right* doesn't bring you to any likely hiding-place in the tunnel, you now try twenty-five paces to the *left* of the dungeon door. This proves equally disappointing, however. The rock is quite solid here, without any secret cavities having been gouged into it. So you sadly continue along the dark tunnel, very soon reaching a series of steps that seem – thankfully – to lead you out of this awful place. You're just about to start climbing them, however, when you hear something shuffling behind you. Is it just a rat – or is it the ghost of one of those former prisoners? *Go to 69*.

Delete the top number in your score card's ♥ column to show that you have one less chance after this haunting. Go next to 51.

43

Having quickly ascended these stone steps, your little party soon finds itself entering a huge hall full of dark shadows. 'So I was right about that underground passage!' Mr Drabb exclaims delightedly. 'It *did* bring us to the main part of the castle! Look, there are some more stone steps through that little arch in the corner over there. They must lead to the castle's upper storeys.

I suggest we climb right to the top first and then make our way methodically back down to this ground floor.'
Go to 102.

44

It's more the lashing rain than curiosity or desire that eventually forces you all to that tower door. For yet another fork of lightning crackles down from the sky, heralding the fiercest downpour yet. Rushing up to the sinister-looking arched door, though, you still half hope that it won't open. But it does – the slow creaking of the hinges echoing all the way to the top of the dingy tower! ***Go to 55***.

45

This time *all three of you* prepare to brave the storm. You can't put it off any longer! Mr Drabb is just starting to open the door again, however, when you notice a large iron ring in the tower's stone floor. 'I think I've found the entrance to a tunnel, Mr Drabb!' you call to him excitedly, as you start to pull the ring. 'Yes – look – there's a trap-door built into the floor. Help me lift it right up, will you?' When you've both at last got the heavy stone slab vertical, you see that you were right. There's a series of rough steps underneath, leading deep into the ground! *Go to 100*.

46

Walking across to this nearest cooking pot, you and Mr Drabb stand either side of it, ready to try to lift it. But it proves even heavier than it looks and, although you manage to keep your side just off the ground, Mr Drabb immediately drops his side again. He hops back in a funny little dance as it very nearly lands on his foot! It seems that you're not the only one to have found this sight rather amusing, though. For you think you can just detect sniggering coming from a little way behind you. Nervously biting your lip, you slowly turn round to see if it was just your imagination . . . *Go to 31*.

Delete the top number in your score card's ♡ column to show that you have one less chance after this haunting. Go next to 106.

48

'Don't lean too hard against that parapet, will you?' Mr Drabb warns as you wait for another glimpse of those caves. 'The stone is crumbling quite badly up here and it all looks very unsafe. Indeed, I think we should leave the top of the tower now. It's a pity, but there are clearly no goblets to be found here!' *Go to 32.*

You chose Cheerful to lead the way in the hope that his keen nose might be able to pick up some of the scent you would have left during your exploration of the island. Although you have to admit, *keen* is not a word that seems very applicable to Cheerful! Nevertheless, he starts to sniff his way slowly through the mist, you and Mr Drabb keeping close behind him. ***Go to 150.***

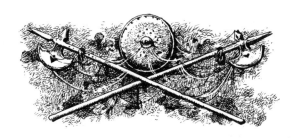

50

'Perhaps we should have tried fifteen paces the *other way*,' you remark after you have both thoroughly tested the wall here. You were hoping to find a part that sounded hollow but this section is completely solid. As you start to make your way back to the tapestry, however, you notice that it is twitching! 'Oh, it's probably concealing a window and a draught is disturbing it,' Mr Drabb remarks. You're sure he's right about there being a window there. But is the tapestry's movement merely caused by the wind coming through? Feeling very tense, you both draw back a corner of the tapestry to find out. *Go to 77.*

51

You've now used up all the time you'd allowed yourselves to explore the middle floor and so your little party starts to make its way back down to the castle's ground level. As you step off the bottom step of the crumbling stairway, Mr Drabb tells you that this huge ground floor would have been the general purpose area of the castle, probably including the kitchens, well and armoury. 'I suggest we explore it quarter by quarter,' he adds. 'Which quarter would you like us to start with first? This bottom left corner or the bottom right? Or perhaps you would prefer one of the top two corners first?'

If bottom left   *go to 132*
If bottom right *go to 23*
If top left   *go to 84*
If top right   *go to 155*

To your immense relief, you see that there is *nothing* turning the spit. In fact, the spit isn't turning any more – it's perfectly still. 'Oh, I must have left the handle in its up position and it suddenly dropped down again, rotating the spit a little,' Mr Drabb says breezily. He's not quite as casual about it as he pretends, though. For he quickly recommends that you now explore elsewhere on this floor rather than returning to the cooking pots! *Go to 118.*

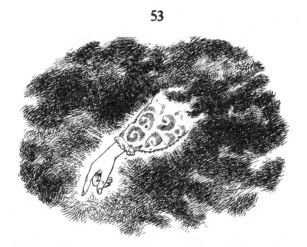

It is a ghostly arm! Delete the top number in your score card's ♡ column to show that you have one less chance after this haunting. Go next to 76.

54

'We must have guessed that instruction incorrectly,' Mr Drabb remarks after you have counted the twenty-five paces to the left. 'Shall we try just five more paces or should we return to the boulder right now so we can start pacing to its right instead?' Well, five more paces wouldn't do any harm, you suppose, and so you agree to walk a little further in this direction. *Go to 29.*

55

Your little group now starts to climb the shadowy steps within the tower – very slowly, very nervously! You must be about a third of the way up the spiral stairway when you come across a narrow passage leading off to the left. And there's a second one, a few steps higher, leading off to the right. You wonder whether you should explore either of these . . . or just keep going to the top of the tower. Which way will you decide on?

If passage to left   **go to 163**
If passage to right   **go to 83**
If continue to top   **go to 3**

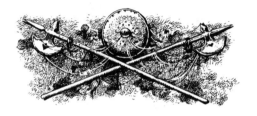

56

You suggested Mr Drabb lead the way ashore for *two* reasons. First, because he would presumably have no objections if he doesn't have any fears about the island. And, second, because you certainly didn't want to lead the way yourself! 'See that tiny pebble cove over there,' the fisherman announces gruffly, pointing straight ahead. 'That's where I'm going to land you. It's the only place you *can* land on the island. The shore is just sheer cliff everywhere else. We should reach the cove in another five minutes or so. That's always assuming that the boat doesn't have its bottom ripped out by the rocks, of course!' *Go to 141.*

Delete the top number in your score card's ♡ column to show that you have one less chance after this haunting. Go next to 24.

Go next to 24.

58

You chose to hurry to the *right* of the steps because you know that the cliff edge isn't very far to the left. You don't want to risk running blindly over it in this lashing rain! Suddenly, though, you rather wish you had gone in the other direction. For you're sure you can see something hovering in the air slightly ahead of you; something white and ethereal! 'Oh, that's just an optical illusion produced by the rainstorm,' Mr Drabb says quickly, trying to reassure you, although his voice sounds far from convinced. 'It's probably just the reflection of the moon or something . . .' *Go to 5.*

59

You nominated Cheerful to lead the exploration into these eerie shadows because of his keen sense of smell. He might be able to sniff out something that you or Mr Drabb would miss. At least, that's what you *pretended* your reason was for suggesting that Cheerful go first. Your *real* reason – or your main reason, anyway – was that you wanted to avoid going first yourself! *Go to 121.*

60

You're examining this window recess in the middle when you suddenly leap back from it in fright. There was another flash of lightning outside and you're

positive you glimpsed a knight on horseback near where it struck the ground! Or was this just because your eyes were dazzled by the lightning? There probably wasn't really anything there at all. But just to make sure, you peer down at that same shadowy spot again, waiting for the lightning to strike a second time . . .
Go to 28.

61

'Oh, this is just a waste of time without more information!' Mr Drabb suddenly exclaims after you have all counted the twenty-five paces and thoroughly searched around for any goblets that might be hidden there. It seems that someone else thinks you're wasting your time as well! For you suddenly hear what sounds like sniggering a short way above your heads. You all slowly raise your eyes, praying that this sniggering is just a trick you're hearing of the fierce wind up here . . .
Go next to 11.

62

Your fears appear to be justified, for you eventually reach two very sturdy and heavily-bolted doors: one built into the rock on the left side of the passage and one on the right. Which door will you try?

If door on left   *go to 89*
If door on right   *go to 15*

63

Since you don't have a map, you'll just have to hope that this *is* the right set of steps for the cove. You don't really have any other choice! Your little party hasn't descended many more of the steps, however, when you suddenly feel a strong gust of wind on the back of your neck. There shouldn't be anything strange about that. There are plenty of strong gusts up here. But this one feels rather warmer than the others . . . as if it's someone's breath! Hoping that this warmth is just a figment of your imagination, you slowly turn round to see if anyone – or any*thing* – is behind you. **Go to 168.**

Delete the top number in your score card's 👻 column to show that you have one less chance after this haunting. Go next to 124.

65

This chest on the right is also crammed with decaying clothes – but is there a goblet hidden amongst them as well? Unfortunately, not. You and Mr Drabb feel right down amongst the clothes, checking every single millimetre of the chest, but all you have to show for your efforts is a horrible green powder on your hands! You've just turned your attention to the chest in the middle, finding musty clothes in this one as well, when you have a strong sense that someone is watching your activity. Feeling very anxious, you raise your heads from the chest, only hoping that you are mistaken . . . *Go to 21.*

66

You help Mr Drabb remove the helmet section from the suit of armour and then tensely hold your breath while he reaches down inside the neck. 'That's about as far as my arm will go, I'm afraid,' Mr Drabb says with a sigh. 'It looks as if I was wrong about one of the goblets being hidden in here. Hang on a minute, though! What's this I can feel?' You hold your breath a second time as he very carefully eases his arm out – but then you suddenly let it go again. For clasped in his fingers, there's a beautiful golden goblet!

Well done! Record this find in your score card's 🏆 column. Go next to 51.

67

You were right about the secret cavity! A small square of the stone wall comes out with the ring as Mr Drabb tugs it, exposing a deep hole there. You can't wait to feel inside the hole but your first task must be to help Mr Drabb up from the dungeon floor. He fell flat on his back when the stone surround suddenly came away with the ring. But wasn't it worth it! For as you both now excitedly feel around inside the cavity, your hand touches what feels very like the stem of a goblet. And a goblet is exactly what it proves to be – a goblet of gleaming gold!

Well done! Record this find in your score card's 🏆 *column. Go next to 123.*

68

Of course, you know that neither you nor Mr Drabb *has* a map. But you're hoping that he might have temporarily forgotten this, keeping you company just a few

seconds longer while he searches his pockets! Just at that moment, though, you're both distracted by the sound of jingling bells from the other side of the hall. Has Cheerful just collided with an old musical instrument lying on the floor – or is it the ghost of a jester who once entertained at the banquets? Trembling, Mr Drabb shines his torch in that direction to find out . . .
Go to 153.

69

Delete the top number in your score card's ♡ column to show that you have one less chance after this haunting. Go next to 43.

70

Your pulse slows down a fraction on seeing that the suit of armour is quite motionless. If it *did* suddenly come to life, at least it's not alive now! But perhaps it was just that one of its metal arms dropped a little after you had disturbed it. Yes, that was surely the explanation for the creaking. Just in case it wasn't, though, you and Mr Drabb decide not to continue with your examination of the rusty figures! *Go to 51.*

71

You decide that you don't have time to investigate the cave, though, worried that you'll miss the fisherman. He's due to return to the cove in just ten minutes and you remember his warning that he wouldn't wait! Fortunately, you soon reach those cliff steps again . . . but time is running out fast. If the fisherman keeps to his word and doesn't hang around for you, it's touch and go whether you'll catch him! *Go to 12.*

72

Your little party carefully descends the steep slope that leads to the chapel, thankful that the rain has eased off a little. The detour proves a waste of valuable time, though, because you find nothing either in the eerie ruin itself or in its even eerier graveyard. You now prepare to make your way back up that slope – *but where's it gone?* The rain has suddenly been replaced with something even worse: a thick mist! 'We're just going to have to trust to luck to get us back to the cove,' Mr Drabb says anxiously. 'Who would you give the best chance of guessing the way correctly?'

> *If Mr Drabb*   go to 20
> *If yourself*   go to 125
> *If Cheerful*   go to 49

Delete the top number in your score card's ♥ column to show that you have one less chance after this haunting. Go next to 118.

Go next to 118.

74

'Well, I don't think we can give any more time to this top level,' Mr Drabb says after you've spent a good half-hour on that cold and eerie search. So your little party now descends the narrow corner stairway to the castle's middle floor. 'Looks like this was the banqueting area,' Mr Drabb says, gasping with delight as his torch picks out a huge oak table next to one wall. It's under a tent of cobwebs and badly rotted. He suggests that to save time, the three of you should perhaps split up for this search; one investigating the furniture, one the walls and one the floorboards. He offers *you* first choice!

If furniture   *go to 113*
If walls   *go to 94*
If floorboards *go to 34*

75

When you glance towards the little boat again, you see that it is already well past that pair of cannons. It's travelling quite fast. There must be a strong tide assisting it. 'Hurry up, Mr Drabb!' you shout anxiously. 'The fisherman will have reached the cove in a couple more minutes. We've got to climb down the rest of these cliff steps as quickly as possible!' But those steps number many more than you'd hoped. You climb down and down, following them to left and right, but still you haven't reached the bottom . . . *Go to 124.*

76

Just one more twist of the steps and you finally arrive at the top of the cliffs. There's still much more climbing to do before you reach the castle, but at least the steps aren't so treacherous from now on. As you continue to ascend them, the castle's massive silhouette gradually comes closer and closer above you. It stands there black, jagged and silent against the menacing sky. ***Go next to 154.***

77

Delete the top number in your score card's ♡ column to show that you have one less chance after this haunting. Go next to 74.

78

Cheerful doesn't seem at all concerned that you nominated him to lead the way ashore. All right, he doesn't look deliriously happy about it, but nor does he seem particularly miserable at the prospect. At least, no more miserable than he was before! The impassive droop on his face remains the same as your boat approaches the island's single landing-place. It's a tiny pebble cove squeezed between all the treacherous cliffs. A cove darkened by sinister shadows . . . a cove that seems to be waiting for your arrival there! ***Go to 147.***

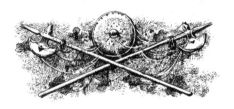

79

The cry, though, is just an excited shriek from Mr Drabb who has been busy investigating the area around the cliffs at the very back of the cove while you and Cheerful were wistfully watching the fisherman's departure from the island. 'Come and look at what I've found in this narrow gash in the rock!' he announces eagerly. 'An old cannonball! When my fingertips first touched it, I obviously hoped that it would be one of the goblets. But a cannonball like this could have a certain value in itself!' As he keeps excitedly turning the heavy metal ball round in his chubby hands, you suddenly notice something strange about it. A small part of its surface has been plugged with a dark-coloured wax! *Go next to 156*.

80

That something is a roll of parchment wrapped round two wooden poles. 'It's an old scroll!' Mr Drabb exclaims excitedly as he carefully separates the poles to open out the crumbling parchment. 'And look, there appears to be a series of clues listed on it! I wonder what they could mean. I would bet my last penny that this is the handywork of the fair Isabella. It's my guess that she wrote down these little picture clues to help herself find the goblets again should her father ever change his mind about forcing her to marry. Well, ultimately, they proved of no avail to poor Isabella, of course. But they might be extremely helpful to us!'

You are now entitled to use the SCROLL on the back flap of this book. Circle the S in the 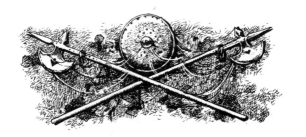 column of your score card so you have a reminder of this whenever the scroll is required. Go next to 106.

81

All you find twenty paces to the right of the cask with the little drawing is a fragment of slate on the stone floor. But then Mr Drabb remembers that slate was a common writing material in Isabella's time and eagerly picks it up to see if there's anything chalked on the other side. There is! But it's not *another* clue, as you had both been hoping. It's simply a stock check of all the casks stored down here. The slate must have been dropped by a careless servant! *Go to 116.*

Delete the top number in your score card's 🐱 ***column to show that you have one less chance after this haunting. Go next to 33.***

83

'Be sure – *sure* – to keep your head well down – *down* – won't you – *you?*' Mr Drabb's voice echoes back at you as he leads you along this mysterious stone passage. 'I've bumped – *bumped* – mine – *mine* – twice already – *dy!*' You're both soon able to straighten up again, though, because the passage is very short. And it leads, in fact, to the open air; to the top of that long crumbling wall which joins the slender tower to the rest of the castle. There is a narrow footway along this wall, but whether it will still be complete for the whole length is very unlikely. Still, you can but hope . . . and so you all start to follow it. ***Go to 128.***

84

'See, I told you we'd find a well somewhere in here!' Mr Drabb exclaims after your little group has made its way towards the top left corner of the vast hall. 'Now, I wonder if Isabella's minstrel boyfriend could have climbed some of the way down this hole to hide one of the goblets? There's just about room for a young agile person to squeeze in there!' You wonder if this is meant to be a hint from Mr Drabb! ***Go to 127.***

85

After a very brief exploration of the cave, you all continue making your way round that huge crag. You at last reach those cliff steps that lead down to the cove where you originally landed. You all race down them because there are now only two minutes to go before the fisherman is due to return! 'What is it, Mr Drabb?' you ask frantically as he suddenly taps you on the shoulder. 'Can't it wait until we're at least down at the cove?' But then you realise that Mr Drabb is on the other side of you. It couldn't have been him who tapped you! So who was it? Trembling, you slowly turn your head . . . *Go next to 112.*

Delete the top number in your score card's ♡ column to show that you have one less chance after this haunting. Go next to 138.

87

The chest in the middle is also full of decomposing clothes – and, unfortunately, nothing but clothes. You were hoping that one of the goblets might have been laid carefully amongst them, but that wasn't to be. Moving over to the chest on the right, you are just as disappointed here. A fair amount of horrible green dust has by now been stirred up by all your rummaging, causing you to start sneezing. Mr Drabb joins in as well. And suddenly so too does someone – or *something* – at the other side of the shadowy hall! *Go to 103.*

88

Your little group keeps going along this lofty footway – but it's as you had feared. You reach a part where the stone has completely fallen away, and it is quite impassible. 'What a shame! We'll have to return to ground level,' Mr Drabb remarks disappointedly, 'and make our way to the rest of the castle from there.' *Go to 138.*

89

To be honest, you would rather have chosen *neither* door, neither left nor right. You're absolutely convinced both have dungeons behind them! But you're well aware that a deep dungeon would have been a perfect hiding-place for one of the goblets. So you help Mr Drabb draw back the rusty bolts on this door . . .
Go to 134.

90

Delete the top number in your score card's ♡ column to show that you have one less chance after this haunting. Go next to 116.

91

Fifteen paces to the right of the quiver brings you all to
an ornamental shield hanging on the wall above two
crossed swords. At least, it probably *was* ornamental.
It's now just a badly-rusted circle of metal! What's
hidden *behind* the shield isn't rusty, though. For gold
doesn't rust. Yes, it's one of those priceless goblets!

***Well done! Record this find in your score card's 🏆
column. Go next to 118.***

92

The upturned pot is extremely heavy but, heaving hard
at one of the handles, you just manage to raise one side a
few centimetres from the floor so that Mr Drabb can
peer underneath. 'Quickly, Mr Drabb!' you implore
him through clenched teeth. 'This thing weighs an
absolute ton! Can you see a goblet under there or not?'
Unfortunately, he *can't* – but as you lower the pot again,

you notice a tiny message scratched on the bottom of it. 'Take a look at this, Mr Drabb,' you tell him excitedly. 'It says that a goblet is hidden in one of the caves on the island. If only it also said *which* cave!' **Go next to 118.**

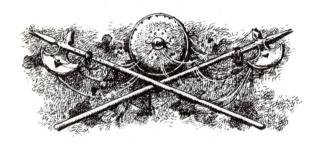

93

Since you can't find anything unusual about the wall here, you decide to try walking twenty paces to the right of the tapestry instead. You're just feeling your way back to it, however, when the centre of the tapestry suddenly starts to shine. 'I'm sure there's nothing to be alarmed about,' Mr Drabb says, somewhat uneasily. 'There's probably a window behind the tapestry and that bright light coming through was just another flash of lightning.' You won't accept this explanation, though, until you've confirmed that there *is* a window behind the tapestry. So you tentatively draw back a corner of the musty hanging . . . **Go next to 77.**

94

Exactly as you did at the level above, you very carefully and slowly run your hands along the crumbling stone walls, feeling into all the nooks and crannies. The only difference here is that this time you're all on your own! A few minutes of this solitude is as much as you can stand, and you wrack your brains trying to think of an excuse to call out to the other two across the gloomy hall. You want to check that they're still there! What can that excuse be, though? You must *have* an excuse. You've got much too much pride to admit that it's just because you're desperate to hear their voices! ***Go next to 8.***

The hole is very close to the island's cliff edge and so you and Mr Drabb decide to keep following this edge round. This way, you're bound to reach the cove *eventually* – the only question is, will it be before the fisherman has given up waiting for you there? Your arranged meeting time is now less than half an hour away! Fortunately, you at last reach the steps leading down to the cove. But there are now less than *five* minutes left. If you don't really hurry, you could be stuck on this terrible island for ever! *Go to 124.*

Delete the top number in your score card's ♥ ***column to show that you have one less chance after this haunting. Go next to 74.***

97

You and Mr Drabb remove the heavy head section
from this suit of armour so he can reach right down
inside it. But, sadly, he fails to find anything there. He
then tries the suit of armour on the right – but that too
proves disappointing. 'Do you think it's worth bother-
ing with the last one?' he asks, rather dispiritedly.
You're not really paying him attention, though, distracted by a faint clinking sound you can hear coming
from behind you. For a brief moment, you hope that it
might just be Cheerful's name disc clinking against his
collar – but then you remember that he doesn't have a
disc and collar on his neck! You take a deep, nervous
breath as you slowly turn your head . . . *Go next to 42.*

98

Mr Drabb leaps out of the boat the moment you reach
the little cove – but you and Cheerful are more hesitant
about it. 'Are you getting out or not?' the fisherman

demands, anxious to row straight out of the cove again. 'You crazed folk might like it 'ere but I certainly don't!' As you gingerly put a foot ashore – making your first acquaintance with this sinister island – you make sure that the fisherman will come back for you. 'Gave you my word, didn't I?' he snaps. 'Yes, *I'll* certainly be here all right. The question is – will you?' *Go to 27.*

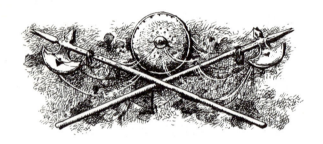

99

Mr Drabb is just telling you not to be so silly about the cliff steps, insisting that they will of course return to the point from which they started, when he suddenly stops mid-sentence. 'Is it just the wind rustling the grass,' he asks, turning rather pale, 'or can you hear music up there above us? To be honest, it sounds like someone plucking a lute! That's just the sort of instrument that Isabella's minstrel boyfriend would have played! Oh, stop being so fanciful, George,' he suddenly chides himself as you all start to lift your eyes. 'Of course it's just the wind . . . ' *Go to 143.*

100

'Fascinating!' Mr Drabb remarks as you all stare down the dark steps. 'This tunnel will almost certainly lead to the main part of the castle, as an alternative route to the battlements. Well, I suggest we take this route ourselves. Not only will the tunnel keep us much drier than going outside, but it would surely have been a perfect hiding-place for one or more of the goblets! What do you think?' *Go to 129*.

101

If there *hadn't* been anywhere to shelter either to the left or the right of the steps, then you would have had to come all the way back again, ending up even wetter than you already are! This is why you decided to keep going for the castle. You have to climb fairly slowly, though, because the worn stone steps, which were slippery enough before the rainstorm, are now absolutely treacherous! You're just about to glance round to make sure Cheerful is keeping up with you when you notice that he is actually at your side. So what's that padding sound you can hear a dozen or so steps behind you? Feeling very tense, you slowly and nervously look over your shoulder to find out . . . *Go next to 47.*

102

You're all panting by the time you finally reach the top of this cramped twisting stairway; Cheerful's face hanging even closer to the floor than usual! 'This would have been the living quarters,' Mr Drabb explains enthusiastically as he leads the way out into a large, dark hall. He shines his torch around, the light catching on rotting pieces of furniture and mouldy wall hangings. Even though you can now hear the fierce storm again outside, there's still a strange silence mingling with these dusty shadows. 'Well, which one of us would you like to lead the exploration?' Mr Drabb asks. 'Me, you or Cheerful?'

> **If Mr Drabb**   *go to 22*
> **If yourself**   *go to 133*
> **If Cheerful**   *go to 59*

103

'W-what is it, Mr Dr-Drabb?' you say, taking a deep gulp as he points his torch in the direction from where you heard the sneeze. The trembling beam shifts from left to right, finally lighting up a long unhappy-looking face. But it's not the face of a ghost. It's Cheerful's! He too must have been affected by all the dust flying around and so quietly waddled all the way over there to avoid it! *Go next to 74.*

Sadly, of course, you don't have a map with you. It suddenly doesn't matter, though, because you're delighted to spot through the mist the approach of the fisherman's little rowing-boat. These steps obviously *do* lead down to the cove after all! The boat is moving very fast, though (it's obviously assisted by a strong tide), and so you must hurry in case the fisherman assumes you didn't make it back to the cove and immediately leaves again. You have gone only a few steps further, however, when you're sure you feel someone blowing on your neck. No, of course you didn't. It's just the wind. Nevertheless, you can't help slowly turning round to make sure . . . *Go to 168.*

105

The length of your straw is only about six centimetres and so you have an anxious moment while you wait to see if Cheerful's is even shorter. Mercifully, it is! And it proves shorter than Mr Drabb's as well. So it's *Cheerful* who must make that unnerving exploration. You would like to feel a bit sorry for him as he plods slowly out of the door – but it's difficult when that drooping face doesn't seem to care much either way! After a while, though, you start to feel rather bad about this. A whole twenty minutes has gone by now and Cheerful still hasn't returned! What could have happened to him? *Go next to 144.*

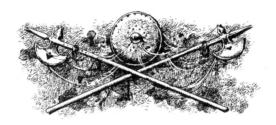

106

Continuing to climb up towards the castle, your little group eventually finds itself right in its menacing shadow. The steep path has brought you to the most westerly end of the sprawling ruin, where looms a slim isolated tower. 'I suppose we must actually *enter* the castle, Mr Drabb?' you enquire nervously as you spot a dark arched door at the base of that tower. 'Of course we must!' he laughs. 'Isabella would surely have hidden *most* of the goblets within its walls. Maybe even all of them!' You notice that his laugh isn't quite as hearty as it was, though. And he seems in no great hurry to lead you up to that door! *Go to 44.*

Delete the top number in your score card's 👻 *column to show that you have one less chance after this haunting. Go next to 118.*

108

These fifteen paces bring you almost to the end of the parapet. A few paces after that, the parapet crumbles away to a sheer six- or seven-metre drop! 'Well, what do we do now?' you ask, bewildered. 'This part of the wall looks much the same as any other part!' Not quite, though. For Mr Drabb notices that one of the large stones that makes up the wall doesn't have any mortar around it. He's just able to fit his fingers either side of the stone and gradually ease it out. There's a small cavity behind . . . and inside that cavity, a gleaming gold goblet!

Well done! Record this find in your score card's 🏆 column. Go next to 24.

109

You've just counted twenty-five paces to the left of the dungeon door when you suddenly hear it slam shut in the darkness behind you. 'That's strange,' Mr Drabb remarks. 'I wouldn't have thought there would be any draught down here.' But the next sound is even harder to try to explain rationally. It sounds like someone moaning . . . and that person seems to be coming straight for you! Fortunately, you soon reach a flight of steps that appear to lead out of this dreadful tunnel. But just before you start to climb it, you can't help casting a nervous glance over your shoulder to see if there's anyone behind you . . . *Go to 69.*

110

Since you don't have a map, though, the glimpse of that pair of caves can tell you very little. For all you know, you could be staring east or west . . . north or south. Indeed, your long climb up here was a bit of a waste of time generally. There are certainly no goblets to be found. Your little party is making its way down again, having descended a dozen or so of the steps, when you are sure you hear someone calling from the top of the tower. With heart pounding, you very slowly climb up a few steps again to investigate . . . ***Go to 86.***

111

'I can only think that this manacle bears *another* instruction,' Mr Drabb says as he handles the huge iron ring in the middle, lifting it from its attachment to the wall. 'I'll try gently scraping off some of the rust with my penknife to see if a message has been scratched underneath.' He has to scrape the rust quite vigorously, though, and you notice that a small area of the stone wall loosens a little as he does this. 'Just give the ring a good tug, Mr Drabb,' you instruct him eagerly. 'I think there might be a secret cavity behind it.' *Go to 67.*

112

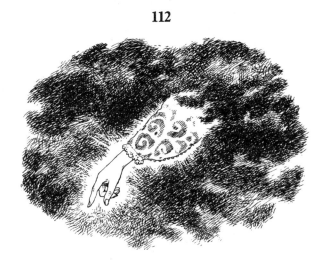

Delete the top number in your score card's ♥ column to show that you have one less chance after this haunting. Go next to 124.

113

The most prominent piece of furniture in this crumbling banqueting hall is obviously that long table. So this is what you walk over to first. Your whole body cringes as you tear away the cocoon of cobwebs so you can see what's underneath. Your heart leaps for a moment as you discover a cluster of goblets – but they're all just pewter ones. Then your eyes rest upon something else that seems promising . . . ***Go to 131.***

114

Unfortunately, of course, you don't have a map with you. 'What do you think caused this huge hole, Mr Drabb?' you ask as you all carefully keep well away from its slippery edge. Thinking hard, he sucks on his cheek for a moment. 'I should imagine it's the sea forcing a tunnel deep underneath,' he replies. 'As the tunnel got bigger, this piece of land above must have simply collapsed into it. If only we *did* have a map of the island!' he adds frustratedly. 'A geological feature as strange as this is sure to have been depicted!' ***Go to 140.***

Why on earth did you volunteer *yourself* to step on to the island first! You suppose it was because you wanted to dispel your silly anxieties about the place. The best way of doing that seemed to be by acting boldly! But as the fisherman starts to steer you towards the one place suitable for landing on the island – a tiny pebbled cove squeezed between all the sheer cliffs – you're very soon regretting your decision. You should have nominated Mr Drabb to step ashore first, given he's so disbelieving of ghosts. Or Cheerful. You don't know whether Mr Drabb's dog believes in ghosts or not – but he surely couldn't look any *more* miserable and so what would it have mattered if he had been given that unpleasant task! ***Go to 147.***

Another passage leads from the far end of the cellar and your little party now hurriedly makes its way along this one as well. Mr Drabb is more confident than ever that these dark, damp tunnels will eventually lead to the main part of the castle. 'That's the part that the cellar would most have to supply,' he explains. 'So the two must surely be linked in some way.' Well, it looks as if you're now about to find out whether he's right. For you reach another flight of stone steps: these, thankfully, leading upwards . . . **Go to 43.**

117

Delete the top number in your score card's ♡ column to show that you have one less chance after this haunting. Go next to 45.

118

You're about to continue your exploration of this ground floor when Mr Drabb suddenly notices the time. You have only an hour left before the fisherman returns to collect you! So, greatly to your relief, your little party finally leaves the sinister castle and steps out into the stormy night again. 'Although time's getting a little short,' Mr Drabb shouts to you above the screaming wind, 'I think before returning to those cliff steps we ought to have a quick look at that ruined chapel over there. If *I* was hiding one of the goblets, I couldn't think of anywhere better to do so!' **Go next to 72.**

119

You eagerly feel all around this window recess on the right, hoping to find a stone tile that's loose. Unfortunately, you don't. The recess is perfectly sound. You're not to be completely disappointed by the window, however, because you discover another minute clue scratched in the stone. And this one's in plain English! It reads: *One of the goblets is hidden on the floor below.* **Go next to 51.**

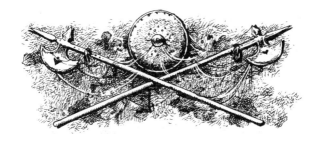

All these casks tell you that the cavern was obviously once the castle's cellar. So you must be nearing the main part after all. And there's even better news – one of the

casks has a funny little chalk drawing on it. Could this be a *secret instruction* left here by Isabella, reminding her to walk a certain number of paces away from the cask?

If you have circled the S in the ⬛ column, you may consult the SCROLL accessory now to find out this drawing's secret instruction. If you haven't, you'll have to guess what you should do:

    If walk 20 paces to left   go to 7
    If walk 25 paces to right   go to 135
    If walk 20 paces to right   go to 81

121

Cheerful starts to sniff his way across the huge rotting floor, you and Mr Drabb following closely behind him with your torches. His progress is very slow. You're not sure whether this is because he is being very thorough – or just very reluctant! Eventually, though, he leads you both right across the shadowy hall, to three large oak chests positioned against the far wall. ***Go to 146.***

122

Your little party hasn't felt its way much further from the window when you hear tapping coming from that direction. You feel your heart start to pound, but Mr Drabb tells you that it's probably just a branch blowing against the glass. There's just one thing wrong with this theory. There *isn't* any glass, of course, in these castle windows. Oh, and another little thing. It would be a very strange tree that had managed to grow up to this height! Terrified, you return to the window, praying that there's a more realistic explanation for the tapping there . . . ***Go to 96.***

123

Quite a distance on from the dungeons – or, at least, it *seems* quite a distance in this horrible eerie passageway – your little group reaches another flight of steps. Phew, at last – it seems that you could soon be out of this sinister damp tunnel. For the steps lead steeply upwards again . . . ***Go to 43.***

124

Having finally reached the bottom of the steps, you're just in time to see the fisherman rowing out of the cove. You've missed him! You and Mr Drabb shout desperately after him, but he must be out of earshot because his little boat now disappears into the night. What are you to do? Suddenly, though, the boat reappears and slowly makes its way back to you. The fisherman did hear you after all! You, Cheerful and Mr Drabb soon step into his boat, so relieved to be leaving this terrible place at last. But how many of those precious goblets are you taking away with you? *That's* what really matters!

If you have managed to collect all five golden goblets, congratulations! If the total in your ♟ column is any less than 5, however, try playing the game again (using a fresh score card) to see if you can improve upon your score.

125

You elected *yourself* to try to find the way back to the cove because you were worried that Cheerful would be too slow and Mr Drabb would be too eager. The former could make you completely miss your trip back to the mainland with the fisherman, and the latter could have you striding straight over a cliff! You've led them both quite a way when the mist finally starts to clear a little and you see that you've come part of the way round the base of the huge crag on which the castle stands. The castle's now way above you again, eerie as ever as its soaring towers disappear into the mist. Bringing your eye right down to the bottom of the crag again, you notice that there is a large cave there. You wonder whether you should quickly investigate it.

If yes   go to 26
If no   go to 71

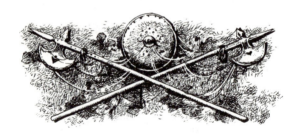

126

Perhaps you should have counted rather fewer paces because you certainly can't find anything that might be a hiding-place near *this* part of the wall! You're just about to retrace some of those paces back to the quiver when you suddenly feel a strong draught on the back of your neck. Either the strength of the storm has blown open the castle's doors . . . or there's something breathing on you! Praying that it's the first explanation, you very slowly turn round with your torch trembling. *Go next to 35.*

127

But if this is meant to be a hint from Mr Drabb, it's a hint you firmly ignore. Especially since you suddenly hear a strange moaning sound coming from down the well! It could just be the distorted echo of your voices, you suppose, but to be absolutely sure, you apprehensively shine your torch down there . . . *Go next to 107.*

128

You all proceed very slowly through the storm along this lofty footway, conscious that this might have been the very part from which Isabella slipped on that fateful night! Cheerful soon discovers something to make you forget these macabre thoughts, however. He even gives a small bark at his discovery! It's a funny little picture chiselled into the stone walkway. 'This could well be a secret instruction carved by Isabella,' Mr Drabb

proclaims excitedly, 'instructing how many paces she should walk from here to find one of the goblets!'

If you have circled the S in the *column, you may consult the SCROLL accessory now to find out this picture's secret instruction. If you haven't, you'll have to guess what to do:*

If walk 30 paces to left	*go to 2*
If walk 25 paces to left	*go to 175*
If walk 25 paces to right	*go to 61*

129

You haven't descended far down the eerie steps when this underground tunnel suddenly splits into two separate branches. One branch goes to the left and the other to the right. You and Mr Drabb both scratch your heads, wondering which you should follow.

Which will you decide on?
  If left branch   go to 159
  If right branch   go to 13

130

Suddenly, the glow appears again. But it's not a ghost — it's just the regular flashing beam from a distant lighthouse! Although you're greatly relieved by this, the episode proves a little disquieting. It shows that deep down Mr Drabb isn't quite as dismissive of the idea of ghosts inhabiting the island as he would like to pretend! *Go to 76.*

131

It's a tiny crest  scratched into the table! What particularly excites you about it is that it's at a place just to the left of the table's centre. This is exactly where Isabella would have sat during the banquets, right at her father's side! But if this is one of her secret instructions, to what does it refer? It's then that you notice three deep slit windows directly opposite on the other side of the shadowy hall. Was the crest to remind Isabella that she had hidden a goblet in one of these?

If you have circled the B in the  *column, you may consult the BOOK OF CRESTS accessory now to find out which window recess you should examine. If you haven't, you'll have to guess:*

   If left   go to 10
   If middle   go to 60
   If right   go to 119

132

Unfortunately, there seems to be nothing in this bottom left corner except the odd stone that's crumbled from the wall and so you now make your way through the near complete darkness to the bottom *right* corner of the vast hall. Here you have rather more luck . . . because you find the remains of the castle's kitchen. Standing in a huge fireplace is an equally huge roasting spit, large enough surely to have turned a whole ox! There are also three massive upturned cooking pots nearby, made of thick cast-iron and reminding you of those ones that witches always sit by in gruesome fairy tales! ***Go next to 142.***

133

You nominated *yourself* to lead the way round this eerie hall because you decided you would much rather be at the very front of the exploration party than at the very back. Who knows *what* might suddenly creep up behind you all! You start off by feeling your way round the crumbling and dusty stone walls, soon coming to a very large decomposing tapestry hanging there. 'Hey, stop a minute!' Mr Drabb exclaims. ***Go next to 161.***

134

Well, it's a dungeon all right! For as you both now tentatively push the door open, your torches immediately light up three large iron rings set into the rough stone wall, about a metre apart. They're manacles! You're inclined to flee this macabre place at once, but Mr Drabb restrains you, pointing out a crest  chalked on to the stone above the manacles. He's sure it's a coded instruction to examine one of the huge iron rings!

If you have circled the B in the 📖 *column, you may consult the BOOK OF CRESTS accessory now to find out which manacle you should examine. If you haven't, you'll have to guess:*

If left manacle	*go to 171*
If middle manacle	*go to 111*
If right manacle	*go to 39*

135

These twenty-five paces to the right bring you all to another wooden cask. 'Mm, I wonder,' Mr Drabb says thoughtfully as he raps its side, then opens the tap at the front. 'Do you see how it's completely empty? Maybe Isabella and her minstrel boyfriend drained it of all its wine and then sealed one of the goblets in the empty barrel!' To find out if his theory is right, he gets hold of the tap and pulls with all his might. His fat little body rolls backwards as the flat end of the cask suddenly comes away. He eagerly jumps back up again, though, and peers inside the opened barrel. *Go next to 173.*

136

You all reach the rough steps. They climb steeply above you, twisting and turning towards the dark summit of the cliffs. As you peer up at the summit, you're sure there are signs of a storm gathering over the island. The clouds have turned to an inky blue and are moving faster and faster across the fading light of the sky. Of course, you hardly need reminding that there was a fierce storm on that night of the tragedy. As if this excursion isn't likely to be chilling enough as it is! *Go next to 6.*

While you are staring at all the chalk markings on the wall, Mr Drabb suddenly becomes interested in a little drawing scratched on the outside of the dungeon door. 'Take a look at this,' he calls to you excitedly. 'I'm

convinced that it's the handywork of Isabella and that it's a secret instruction *to walk a number of paces* from this door!'

If you have circled the S in the ⬗ *column, you may consult the SCROLL accessory now to find out this drawing's secret instruction. If you haven't, you'll have to guess what you should do:*

If walk 30 paces to left	*go to 17*
If walk 25 paces to left	*go to 109*
If walk 25 paces to right	*go to 41*

138

Having finally reached the bottom of the tower again, you all step outside, ready to make your trek to the main part of the castle. But the rain and the wind almost blow you straight back in again. The storm is fiercer than ever! 'Just say the entrance to that main part takes quite a while to find,' Mr Drabb considers, 'we're all going to be soaked to the skin! Perhaps we should send just *one* of us out there to do the searching, so when they've found the entrance, they can hurry back and collect the others!' He picks up three lengths of straw from the floor and offers them to you in his fist. 'Whoever chooses the shortest,' he says, 'is the one that goes!'

Which straw will you take?
If one on left   go to 37
If one in middle   go to 152
If one on right   go to 105

139

'Brilliant!' Mr Drabb shrieks as he shines his torch at the dark object in the hole. 'It's one of the golden goblets!' You're both in for a huge disappointment, though. It's certainly a *goblet* Mr Drabb extracts from the hole – but not a golden one. It's just of cheap pewter! 'Isabella must have been cleverer than we thought,' Mr Drabb says with a sigh. 'It looks as if she left some *false* treasures at the end of her clues as well as genuine ones. They must have been to confuse her father should he ever have gone searching for the goblets!' ***Go to 74.***

140

Since your little party doesn't possess a map, there seems little alternative but to continue trying to *guess* your way through this mist. Mr Drabb proves a lucky guide after all, though, because you eventually reach the cliff steps again. You all frantically dash down them as fast as you can; there being only two minutes to go before your arranged meeting time with the fisherman! Suddenly, though, you can't move, chilled to the spot. You thought you heard someone singing behind you! Is this Isabella's minstrel boyfriend, determined to make sure you never return to this island? ***Go to 64.***

141

Mr Drabb can't wait to leap out of the little boat when the fisherman has rowed you right into the cove. But you and Cheerful are far less eager, taking your time over leaving the boat. As you both watch the fisherman quickly start back for the mainland, you only hope you can trust him to return for you in five hours' time. You rather got the impression that he didn't think there would be much point! You're still watching him grow smaller on that gloomy sea when suddenly there's a cry behind you, making you nearly jump out of your skin . . . *Go to 79.*

142

'Fascinating!' Mr Drabb exclaims as he starts to turn the spit's large wooden handle. 'Absolutely fascinating!' The spit makes an eerie creaking noise as he keeps turning it, though, which seems to echo right through the castle! So you're relieved when he eventually stops, having suddenly noticed a little arrow carved into the spit's handle. It points in the direction of those three upturned cooking pots. Carved there is also a tiny crest , just above the arrow. It looks as if this might well be a secret instruction to inspect one of the pots!

If you have circled the B in the ✎ column, you may consult the BOOK OF CRESTS accessory now to find out which cooking pot you should examine. If you haven't, you'll have to guess:

   If first   go to 46
   If second go to 92
   If third   go to 19

But it is the minstrel's ghost! Delete the top number in your score card's ♡ column to show that you have one less chance after this haunting. Go next to 76.

144

To your great relief, Cheerful's face at last appears through the door! His expression is just as miserable as ever, even though he has *found* something during his expedition. He carries a very small, very old book in his mouth. 'Look,' Mr Drabb remarks on taking the leather-bound book from him, 'the centre page depicts various crests, with what appear to be instructions jotted down beside them. I wonder if this book belonged to Isabella . . . and the instructions relate to where the goblets are hidden!'

You are now entitled to use the BOOK OF CRESTS on the back flap *of this book. Circle the B in the*  *column of your score card so that you have a reminder of this whenever the Book of Crests is required. Go next to 45.*

145

Your trembling immediately stops on discovering that there was a much more rational explanation for the shuffling sound. Mr Drabb was right when he said that the part of the parapet you were leaning against could be unsafe. It has suddenly collapsed! The sound you heard was obviously just the stones slowly crumbling away. *Go to 138.*

146

Having knelt down and opened one of the chests, you find that they are full of musty gowns and robes. Starting to sneeze, you're just about to drop the lid again when Mr Drabb notices a little crest ⚔ scratched on its underside. He wonders if it's a secret instruction, telling you to examine one of the chests further!

If you have circled the B in the 📖 *column, you may consult the BOOK OF CRESTS accessory now to find out which chest you should examine. If you haven't, you'll have to guess:*

   If left chest   *go to 172*
   If middle chest *go to 87*
   If right chest   *go to 65*

147

'Now, you will be sure to come and pick us up again, won't you?' Mr Drabb asks the fisherman when the three of you are all out of his boat and standing on the tiny pebbled beach. 'Promised I would, didn't I?' the fisherman mumbles, nervously glancing round at the darkening cliffs above. 'I'll be 'ere in exactly five hours' time, like I said,' he adds gruffly as he immediately starts to row his little boat out of the cove again. 'But I ain't gonna wait. If you're not 'ere by then, I'll take it that . . . well, don't say I didn't give you fair enough warning about this place!' *Go next to 27.*

You appear to have come out on to the top of a low keep, about a third of the height of the tower. You gaze up at the tower and the crying seagulls circling around it. Mr

Drabb suddenly calls your attention to a little picture whittled into part of the stone parapet. He's sure it's a secret instruction left by Isabella . . . the instruction being to count a certain number of paces from here!

If you have circled the S in the 🗞 column, you may consult the SCROLL accessory now to find out this picture's secret instruction. If you haven't, you'll have to guess what you should do:
  If walk 15 paces to right   go to 36
  If walk 25 paces to left   go to 4
  If walk 15 paces to left   go to 108

149

While you and Mr Drabb are busy discussing the cave, Cheerful is busy actually *investigating* it, constantly sniffing around the damp cavern. You've never seen him look so animated. Perhaps it's because he knows he'll be going home soon! His efforts don't go unrewarded either. For, concealed in a small nook, he suddenly finds one of the golden goblets! Just ten minutes after you've all left the cave, you've reason to rejoice a second time. Cheerful makes another important discovery. He's found you those cliff steps again, the ones that descend to the cove!

Well done! Record this find in your score card's 🏆 *column. Go next to 124.*

After a while, Cheerful suddenly stops at a large boulder on the ground and turns his doleful face towards you both. 'Have you found something, boy?' Mr Drabb asks eagerly, crouching down beside him. 'By Jove, he

has! It's something *chiselled* into the rock. I think it could well be one of Isabella's secret instructions, reminding her to walk a certain number of paces from here!'

If you have circled the S in the ✍ column, you may consult the SCROLL accessory now to find out this picture's secret instruction. If you haven't, you'll have to guess what you should do:

If walk 30 paces to right   go to 169
If walk 30 paces to left   go to 29
If walk 25 paces to left   go to 54

151

Mr Drabb hasn't led you much further up the cliff steps when he suddenly stops. 'What's wrong, Mr Drabb?' you ask with concern. 'Are you out of breath? Perhaps you shouldn't be in *too* much of a hurry.' His rapid breathing is for quite a different reason, though. 'Can you see that strange glow way over there?' he asks tensely, pointing a trembling hand out to sea. 'It keeps coming and going. It's as if something is hovering above the water!' Your eyes nervously follow the direction of his hand, and you anxiously wonder whether you're about to see your first ghost on that dark horizon . . .
Go to 130.

152

The straw you drew is barely five centimetres long! So you anxiously wait to find out the lengths of the other two straws. It's just as you'd feared – both Cheerful's and Mr Drabb's are longer. It's *you* who must make that terrifying expedition! You haven't ventured very far from the tower, however, when you suddenly hear what sounds like someone *weeping* above you. Positive that this is the ghost of the sad Isabella, you hare back to the others. Only when Mr Drabb has opened the tower's heavy wooden door to you and yanked you inside to find out what's wrong, do you dare look outside again to see if the ghost is still up there . . . *Go next to 165.*

153

Delete the top number in your score card's ♡ column to show that you have one less chance after this haunting. Go next to 51.

154

The inevitable suddenly happens. The castle's sleeping silhouette flashes to life, shuddering and angry, as a fork of lightning rents the sky. A moment of quiet follows the blinding zig-zag and then a deluge of rain suddenly sweeps over the island. 'I'm not sure whether we're best to seek shelter or keep going!' Mr Drabb shouts as you both yank up your anorak hoods. 'There might be somewhere to shelter just a little way to the left or right of these steps – then again, there might not. On the other hand, that castle's still a good six hundred metres away. I really don't know what to suggest. Where do *you* think we should hurry?'

> *If to left of steps*   go to 30
> *If to right of steps*   go to 58
> *If on towards castle* go to 101

155

You all reach the top right corner of the hall, having felt your way round the crumbling stone of the cobweb-strewn walls. Mr Drabb was right when he said that you could probably expect to find an armoury somewhere on this huge floor of the hall. For you come upon a number of rusting swords and shields hanging on the wall here and iron quivers full of crossbow arrows. Mr

Drabb suddenly notices that one of these quivers has a tiny picture scratched on it. He wonders if it could possibly be one of Isabella's secret instructions, a golden goblet being hidden just a few paces away!

If you have circled the S in the 📜 *column, you may consult the SCROLL accessory now to find out this picture's secret instruction. If you haven't, you'll have to guess what you should do:*

    If walk 15 paces to right   go to 91
    If walk 15 paces to left   go to 170
    If walk 20 paces to right   go to 126

156

You and Mr Drabb hurriedly gouge out this wax plug, sure that it's to disguise a hole drilled into the cannon-ball. Yes, there *is* a hole underneath and, just as you'd guessed, there's something hidden there. It's a tightly-rolled map of the island!

You are now entitled to use the MAP on the front flap of this book. Circle the M in the 📖 *column of your score card so that you have a reminder of this whenever the map is required. Go next to 27.*

157

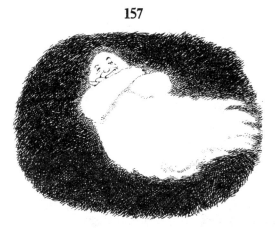

Delete the top number in your score card's 🗲 *column to show that you have one less chance after this haunting. Go next to 88.*

158

You find Mr Drabb scrutinising three suits of armour which are standing next to the wall. 'Take a look at this one's helmet,' he tells you eagerly, pointing to a tiny crest ⌐ scratched on the visor. 'Well, there's exactly the same crest scratched on the helmets of the other two figures! I think it could well be one of Isabella's clues. Perhaps one of these suits of armour hides a goblet!'

If you have circled the B in the ✍ column, you may consult the BOOK OF CRESTS accessory now to find out which suit of armour you should search for a goblet. If you haven't, you'll have to guess:

If left suit	*go to 97*
If middle suit	*go to 66*
If right suit	*go to 18*

159

You're soon wondering if you should have chosen the *other* flight of steps. For the one you chose seems to be endless, continuing down and down into the rocks. At last it reaches a level tunnel but, as you follow this sinister and narrow passageway, you start to have another worry. Mr Drabb might have been wrong in assuming that this was just an alternative route to the rest of the castle. Well, the other branch might have been . . . but perhaps this one has a very different destination. The castle's dungeons! *Go next to 62.*

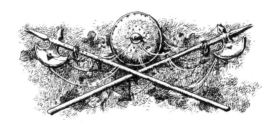

160

You hold your breath as Mr Drabb eagerly thrusts his hand into the barrel of the cannon. You have to hold it even longer because he now inserts his whole arm, reaching deeper and deeper. It looks like he can't feel anything, though. Or can he? For he starts to frown, wiggling his arm a bit. Even Cheerful is beginning to look a little excited. Well, not excited exactly (you're sure that drooping face could *never* look excited!), but at least a tiny bit interested. Unfortunately, though, Mr Drabb's hand *isn't* clutching a goblet when he withdraws it from the cannon. But it is clasping something! *Go next to 80.*

'Have a look at this little corner of the embroidery. It doesn't seem to match the rest of the pattern,' Mr Drabb says as he examines the tapestry closely. 'I'm talking about this tiny feather here. Can you see?

Perhaps Isabella embroidered it on *after* the tapestry was made as a secret instruction; to remind her that one of the goblets was hidden near here!'

If you have circled the S in the ✍ column, you may consult the SCROLL accessory now to find out this embroidered feather's secret instruction. If you haven't, you'll have to guess what you should do:

If walk 15 paces to left   go to 50
If walk 20 paces to left   go to 93
If walk 20 paces to right   go to 25

162

As it turns out, you don't really need a map to confirm whether that silhouette is a chapel. For another flash of lightning momentarily illuminates the island, turning it an angry white and purple, and you glimpse a huddle of gravestones in front of the little building. It was a very eerie huddle, the sight of it sending a shiver right the way down your spine! *Go to 74.*

163

This stone passage is not only narrow but the roof is very low as well, and so you and Mr Drabb both have to keep your heads well down. 'You see, people were quite a bit shorter in those days than we all are now,' Mr Drabb explains, as if he's absolutely fascinated. But you're sure his chatter is just to hide how nervous he feels in the eerie passage! Very soon, though, the passage leads you all out into the open air. *Go next to 148.*

'I f-f-found the entrance,' Mr Drabb says, his voice shaking considerably as he tumbles in through the door, 'but I'm sure s-something f-f-followed me back here. You wouldn't peep out of the door, would you, to see what it is? It's probably just an inquisitive hare or something.' You oblige him, feeling very nervous yourself, opening the door a fraction and peering through the gap . . . *Go to 117.*

Delete the top number in your score card's ♡ column to show that you have one less chance after this haunting. Go next to 45.

166

As it turns out, you find that you don't need a map anyway. For you suddenly make out a little rowing-boat coming towards you past that pinnacle of rock. It must be the fisherman making his way back towards the cove. So these cliff steps are the right ones after all! You shouldn't rejoice too soon, though, because the rowing-boat is approaching quite fast. It must have a strong tide assisting it. At this rate, it will have reached the cove in just another minute or so. What concerns you is that, if you're not down there by then yourselves, the fisherman might not wait! *Go to 124.*

167

It looks as if you might just catch the fisherman after all. For at last you're nearing the bottom of the cliff steps. There's just one or two more bends to go now. Suddenly, though, you all stop dead. You can hear panting from round that next bend. Someone – or some*thing* – is coming up the steps towards you! Nervously gripping Mr Drabb's arm, you only hope that it's the fisherman. But he surely wouldn't dare set foot on this island . . . *Go to 174.*

168

Delete the top number in your score card's 𝔙 column to show that you have one chance less after this haunting. Go next to 124.

169

You'd hoped that these thirty paces to the right would bring you to one of the goblet's hiding-places. They don't, unfortunately – but they *do* bring you back to those cliff steps that lead down to the cove! 'I wonder why Isabella wanted to remind herself where these steps were?' Mr Drabb asks thoughtfully. 'Perhaps she had planned to escape one night and was worried that it might be a night like this where she could easily get lost. So she left lots of secret signposts around!' **Go to 33.**

You wonder whether you should have walked fifteen paces to the right of the quiver instead. You certainly haven't reached any likely hiding-place going in *this* direction. There's just bare wall! You're just about to walk back to the quiver to try that other direction when Cheerful lets out the faintest of woofs. That's most unlike him. He's generally far too miserable to utter any sound at all! Could he have found something? Or is it *bad* news he's trying to convey . . . for you suddenly hear what sounds like sniggering coming from just behind you all. You very slowly turn to look over your shoulder. *Go to 73.*

You and Mr Drabb closely examine the heavy iron manacle on the left, hoping to find perhaps a secret message scratched into it, but there is nothing. 'Well, let's have a look at one of the others,' Mr Drabb suggests, not to be put off. You point out that the crest might have been instructing something very different, though – if, indeed, it was an instruction at all. 'Yes, I suppose you might well be right,' Mr Drabb concedes sadly as he allows you to lead him out of the eerie dungeon again. 'We could just be wasting our time here!' ***Go to 123***.

172

The left chest turns out to be the very one you're looking at now and so you rummage deeper and deeper amongst the clothes. But that's all there seems to be in there – just mouldy and decaying velvets and satins. You suddenly spot a tiny scrap of yellowing parchment near the bottom of the chest, though. 'Look, there's some faded handwriting on it,' Mr Drabb exclaims, excitedly holding it right up to the light of his torch, 'and it bears the signature *Isabella*! It says that three of the goblets are hidden *within* the castle and the other two are hidden somewhere outside it!' ***Go to 74***.

173

'Is there anything there, Mr Drabb?' you ask impatiently as he now inserts his whole head into the large barrel. 'Is one of the goblets inside or not?' Mr Drabb has to disappoint you . . . but he isn't completely empty-handed as he finally withdraws from the barrel. He's found a tiny roll of yellowing parchment in there. 'Ah, so *this* is what Isabella's secret instruction was meant to lead one to!' he exclaims as he unrolls the parchment. 'Or, at least, meant to lead her minstrel boyfriend to! It's a charming love poem she has written for him to sing.' ***Go next to 116.***

174

Delete the top number in your score card's ♡ *column to show that you have one less chance after this haunting. Go next to 124.*

175

You and Mr Drabb exchange excited glances with each other. Could you be about to claim your first goblet? For the twenty-five paces bring you *exactly* to a loose flagstone in the walkway. You help Mr Drabb raise the stone and then eagerly prop it upright for him so his hand can search the deep hole underneath. He extracts not a golden goblet from this hole, though, but a lock of beautiful raven hair. 'It's presumably Isabella's lock,' Mr Drabb says sadly as he decides to return it to its secret place. 'She must have hidden it here for her minstrel boyfriend to find!' *Go to 88.*

176

But soon you and Mr Drabb are chuckling heartily with relief. Maybe there's even the tiniest of chuckles from Cheerful too. Or, at least, a wry grin. For a rabbit has suddenly appeared round the bend in the steps! You're so pleased at this sight, however, that you temporarily forget the hurry you're in. 'Come on, you two!' you shout urgently, suddenly realising. 'If we're not careful, the fisherman will have come and gone!' *Go to 124.*

Collect all four titles in this series:

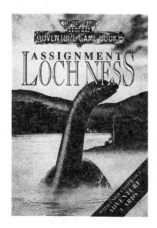

And have you also read Stephen Thraves'
Super Adventure Game Books
with separate cards and special dice?